I0467771

Limited Fine Art Photographs

Decades of being around accomplished artists producing absolutely phenomenal quality work has taught that we are capable of greatness. It is possible to meet our destiny and become it. Experiencing excellence done with such apparent magical ease and humble selfless gratification is the inspiration for this original photography. It is an expression of freedom.

Being colorblind gives an advantage when composing black & white... less confusion. This collection selected from thousands of captures. All images were framed in the camera and presented without edits, genuine as seen through the lens. RAW conversion applied by proprietary panchromatic process.

Fine art prints available from original files.

info@ BeachNoise.com

Joseph Fleming

0351

0531

0705

0780

0826

0920

0938

1581

1608

1784

2180

2467

2495

2631

3147

3359

3714

3720

3799

3943

4070

4099

4193

4265

4533

4879

5492

5541

5750

5784

5844

6095

6176

7182

7339

7656

7939

8173

8345

8470

8471

8889

9024

9353

9430

9975

9980

9992